COLLECTIVE SOUL

TRANSCRIBED BY MATT SCHARFGLASS, NEAL JOHNSON AND MARK NEWMAN

PROJECT MANAGER: AARON STANG
TRANSCRIPTION EDITOR: COLGAN BRYAN
TECHNICAL EDITOR: GLYN DRYHURST
ENGRAVER: ROSARIO ORTIZ

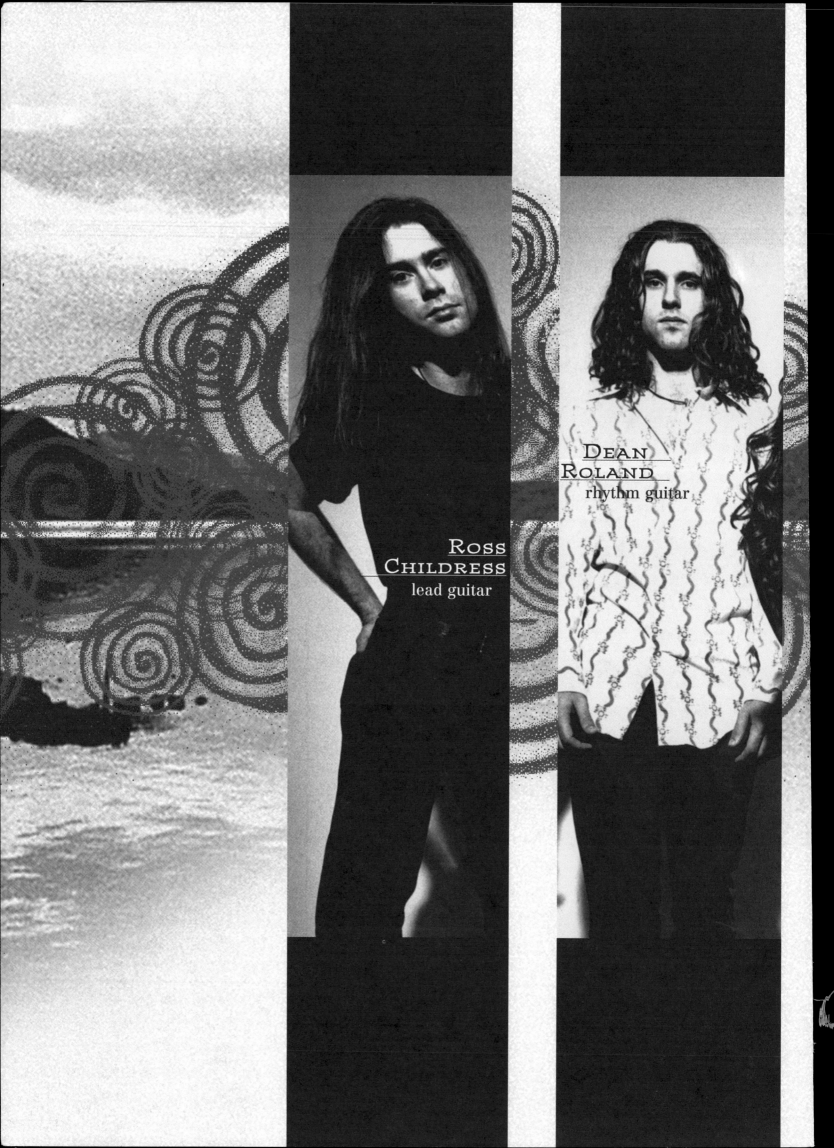

ROSS
CHILDRESS
lead guitar

DEAN
ROLAND
rhythm guitar

ED
ROLAND
lead vocals, guitars

WILL
TURPIN
backing vocals, bass

SHANE
EVANS
drums

SIMPLE

Music by ED ROLAND & ROSS CHILDRESS
Lyrics by ED ROLAND

6

Verses 1 & 2:
w/Riff A (Gtrs. 1 & 2, 2 times) & Rhy. Fig. 2 (Gtr. 3, 4 times)

1. Tan - gle up your twist - ed tongue.__ It's sim - ple.
2. *See additional lyrics*

*Gtr. 4

Rhy. Fill 1

mf

*Gtr. 4 play Verse 2 only.

Mes - mer - ize__ your ev' - ry - day.__ It's sim - ple.

w/Rhy. Fill 1 (Gtr. 4, 4 times, Verse 2 only)

Hey,__ hey, can't you see? Love is all__ that you should need.

Gtrs. 1 & 2

Simple - 9 - 3
PG9536

Hey,___ hey, can't you see?

Chorus:

Ease___ your___ trou - bled mind.___ Let love seek and let___ love___ find. It's

sim - ple.

8

12

w/Rhy. Figs. 4 *(Gtrs. 1 & 2, 10 times)* **& 4A** *(Gtr. 3, 10 times)*

Want a sim-ple lit-tle thing to push on me? Want a sim-ple lit-tle thing to *shove* on me? Want a sim-ple lit-tle thing to touch on me? Want a sim-ple lit-tle thing to love on me? *Yeah!*

Gtr. 4   **Riff D**

f
pick sl.   *grad. bend*

w/Riff D *(Gtr. 4, 4 times, simile)*   E   All gtrs.

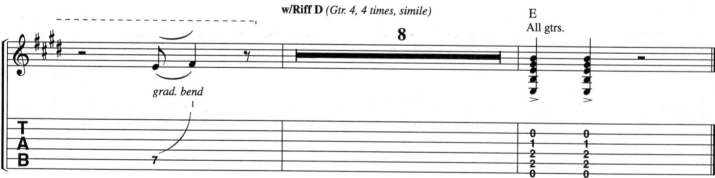

grad. bend

Verse 2:
Pry into combative times. It's simple.
Forfeit all your lush concerns. It's simple.
Hey, hey, don't you care?
Love is all that you should share.
Hey, hey, don't you care?
(To Chorus:)

UNTITLED

Music and Lyrics by
ED ROLAND

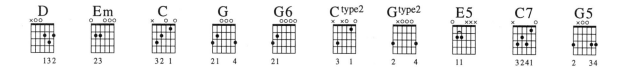

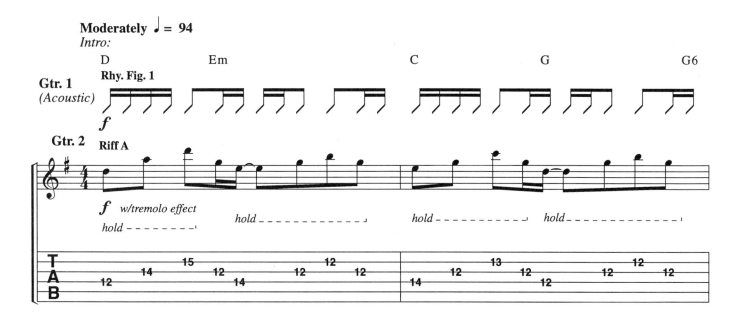

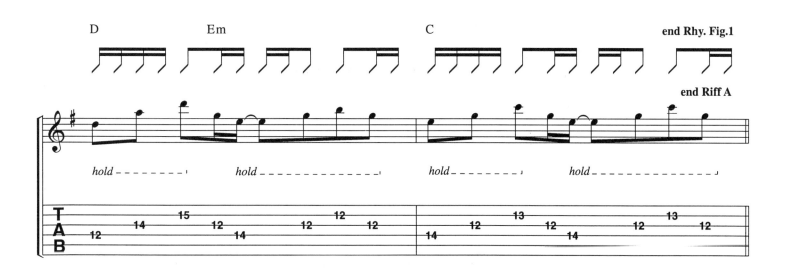

Untitled - 10 - 1
PG9536

(Gtrs. 1 & 2 tacet)

Verse:

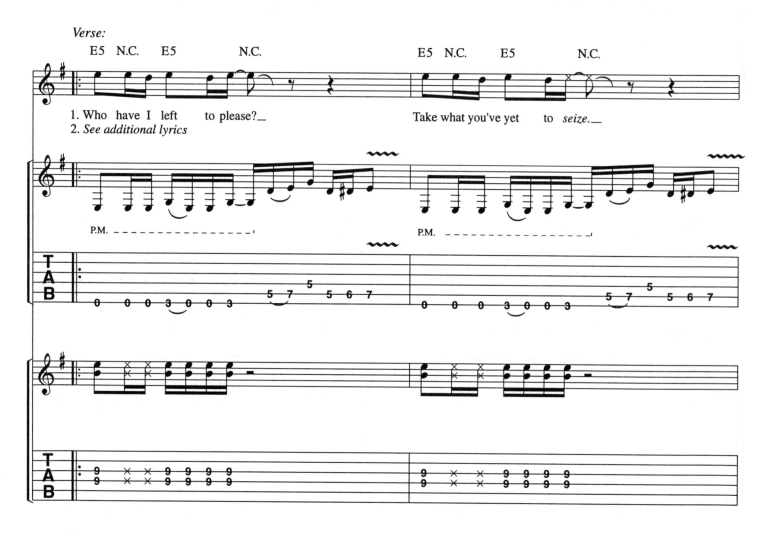

1. Who have I left   to please?__   Take what you've yet   to *seize.*__
2. *See additional lyrics*

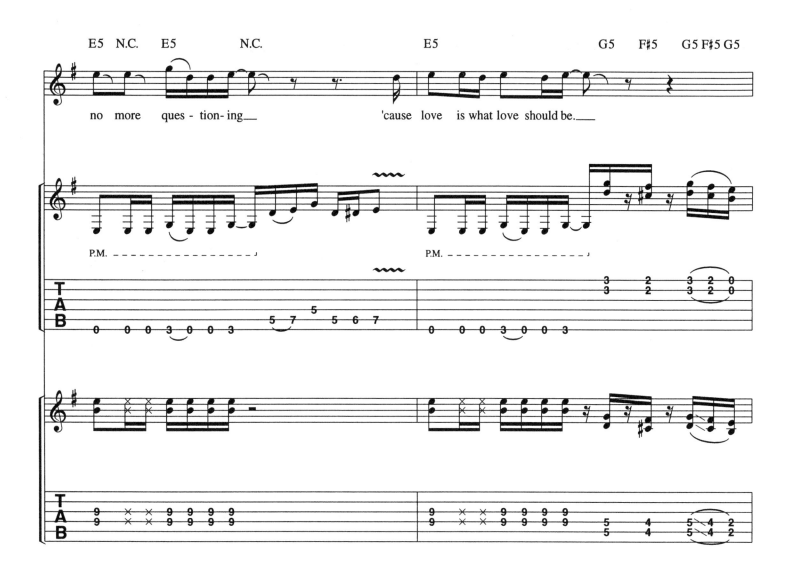

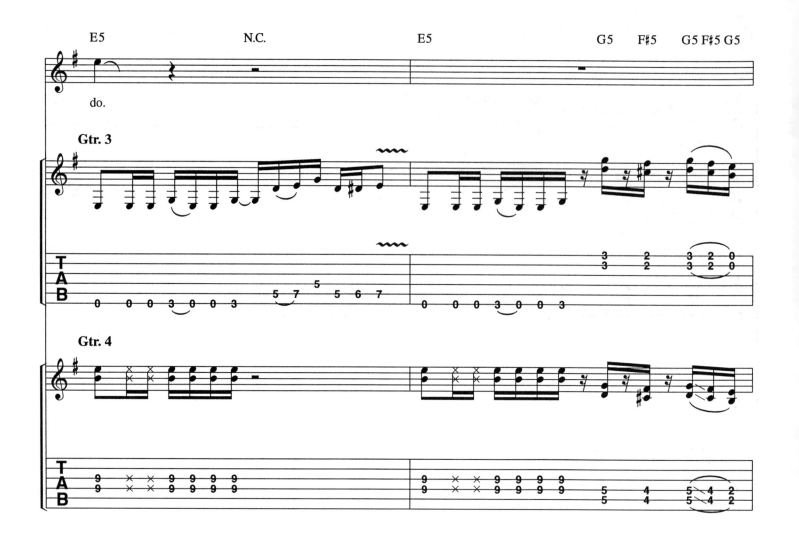

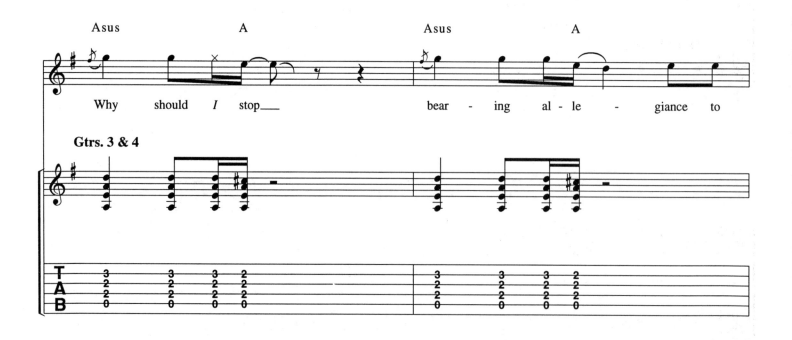

Chorus:
w/Rhy. Fig. 1 *(Gtr. 1)* & Riff A *(Gtr. 2) Both 2 times*

Gtrs. 3 & 4
Rhy. Fig. 2

I don't be-lieve__ in the sor - c'rers or the preach - ers.

Bkgrd. Voc. Fig. 1

Oh, I don't be - lieve.___ I won't be - lieve.__

I just be - lieve__ in you.__

I just be - lieve.__

w/Bkgrd. Voc. Fig. 1 & Rhy. Fig. 2 *(Gtrs. 3 & 4)*

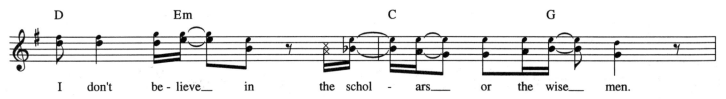

I don't be-lieve___ in the schol - ars___ or the wise___ men.

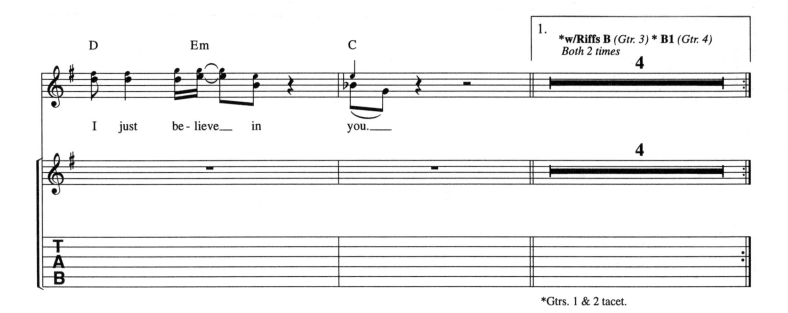

1.
*w/Riffs B *(Gtr. 3)* *** B1** *(Gtr. 4)*
Both 2 times

I just be-lieve___ in you.___

*Gtrs. 1 & 2 tacet.

2.
N.C. (E5)
†Gtrs. 3 & 4

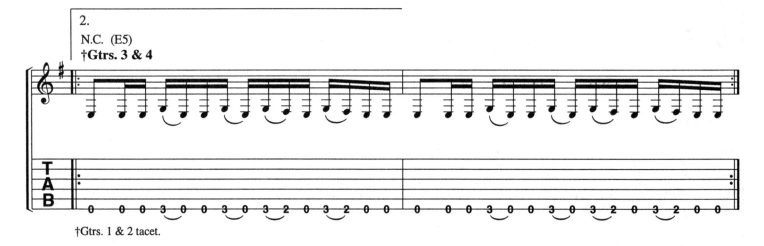

†Gtrs. 1 & 2 tacet.

Interlude:
E5

Gtr. 3
Gtr. 4

decresc.

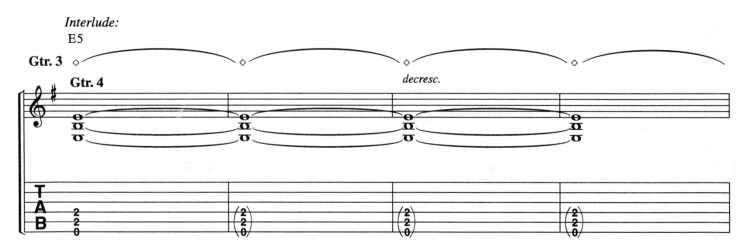

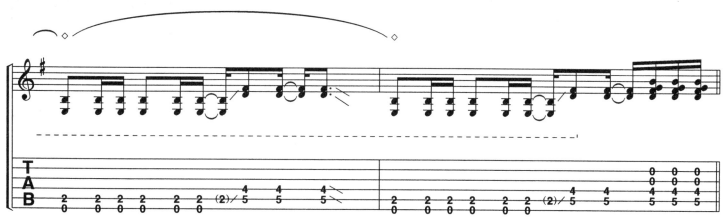

Guitar Solo:

20

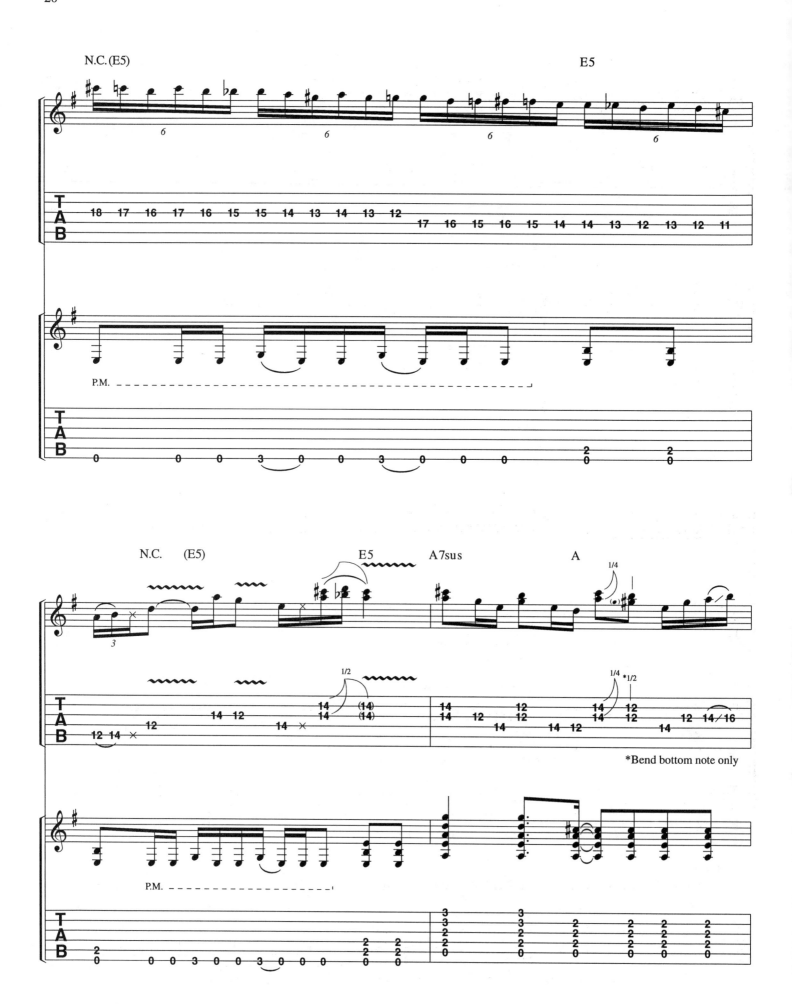

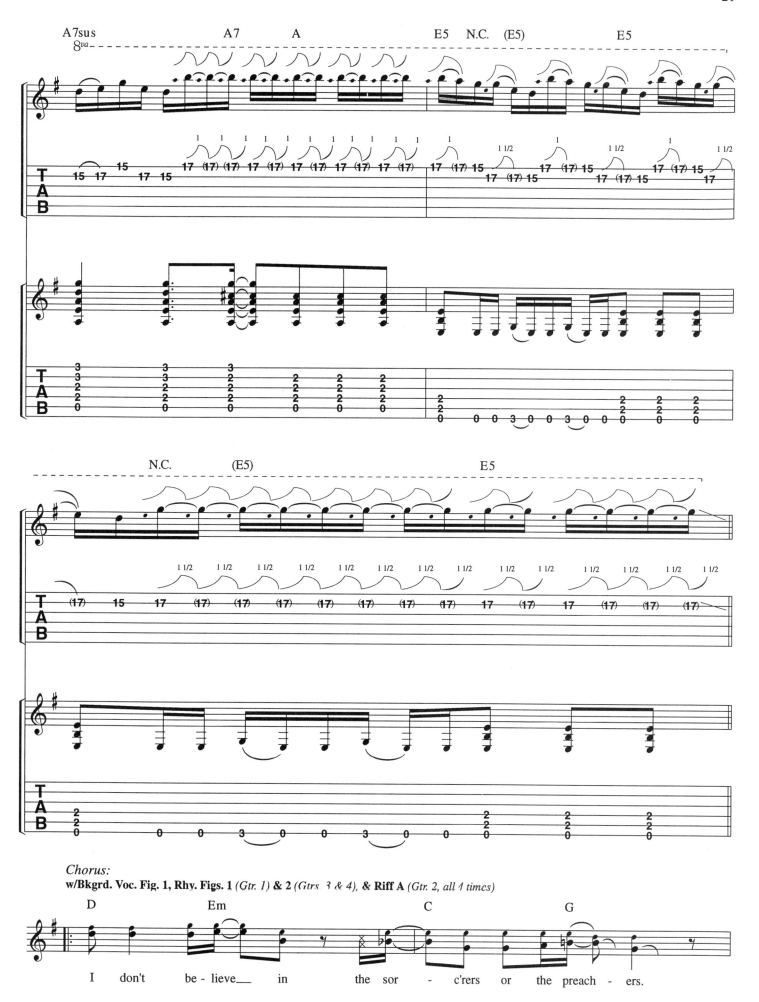

Chorus:
w/Bkgrd. Voc. Fig. 1, Rhy. Figs. 1 *(Gtr. 1)* & 2 *(Gtrs. 3 & 4)*, & Riff A *(Gtr. 2, all 4 times)*

I don't be-lieve___ in the sor - c'rers or the preach - ers.

Verse 2:
What have I left to prove?
I speak all the words you choose.
Confine me in walls of truth
'Cause love does what love should do.
No more sentence.
All of my pain has been freed.
Why should this end?
Your mercy's all I need.
(To Chorus:)

THE WORLD I KNOW

Music by ED ROLAND & ROSS CHILDRESS
Lyrics by ED ROLAND

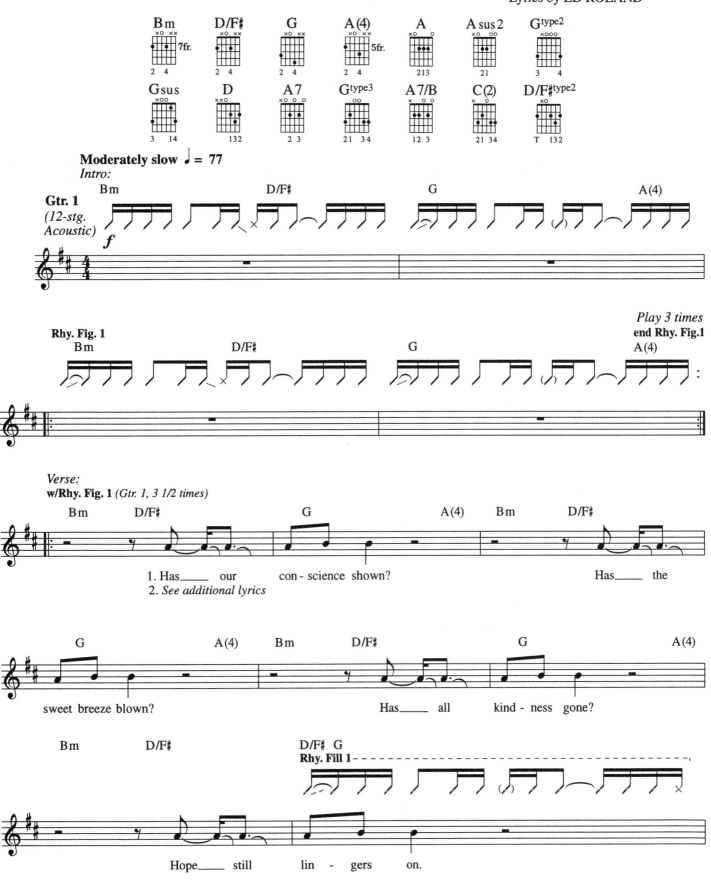

24

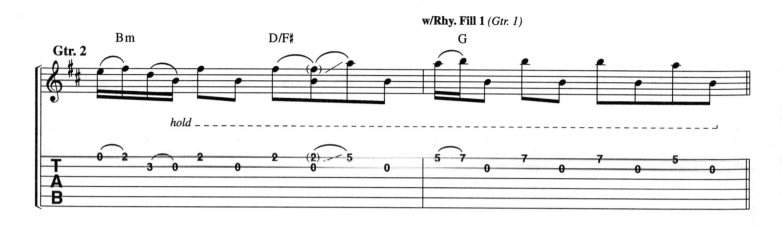

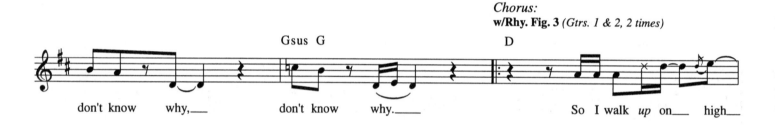

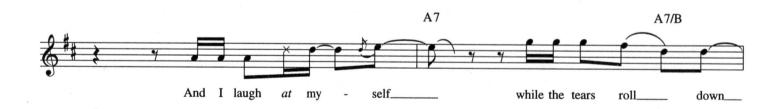

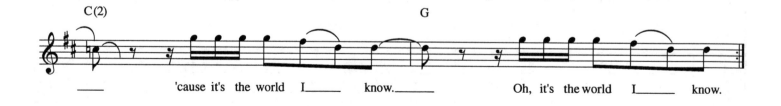

Verse 2:
Are we listening to hymns of offering?
Have we eyes to see that love is gathering?

Pre-Chorus:
All the words that I've been reading
Have now started the act of bleeding
Into one, into one.
(To Chorus:)

SMASHING YOUNG MAN

Music and Lyrics by
ED ROLAND

your po-si-tion,___ oh, don't think___ I did-n't lis-ten.___

Rhy. Fill 1

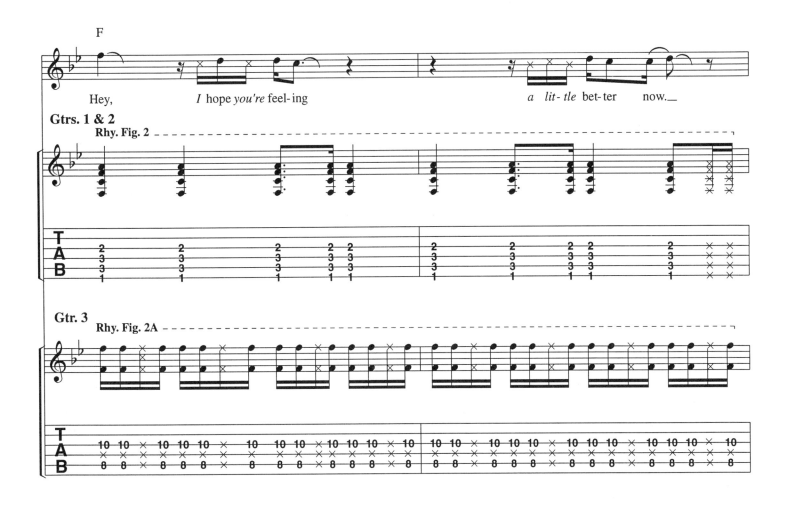

Hey, I hope you're feel-ing a lit-tle bet-ter now.___

Gtrs. 1 & 2

Rhy. Fig. 2

Gtr. 3

Rhy. Fig. 2A

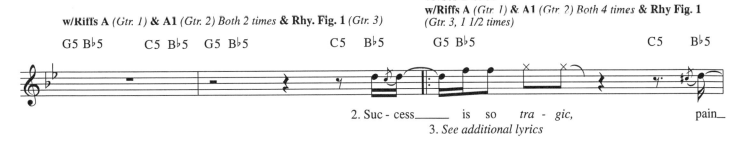

Verses 2 & 3:
w/Riffs A *(Gtr. 1)* & A1 *(Gtr. 2) Both 4 times* & Rhy Fig. 1
(Gtr. 3, 1 1/2 times)

w/Riffs A *(Gtr. 1)* & A1 *(Gtr. 2) Both 2 times* & Rhy. Fig. 1 *(Gtr. 3)*

G5 B♭5   C5 B♭5 G5 B♭5   C5 B♭5   G5 B♭5   C5 B♭5

2. Suc-cess___ is so *tra-gic,* pain___
3. *See additional lyrics*

30

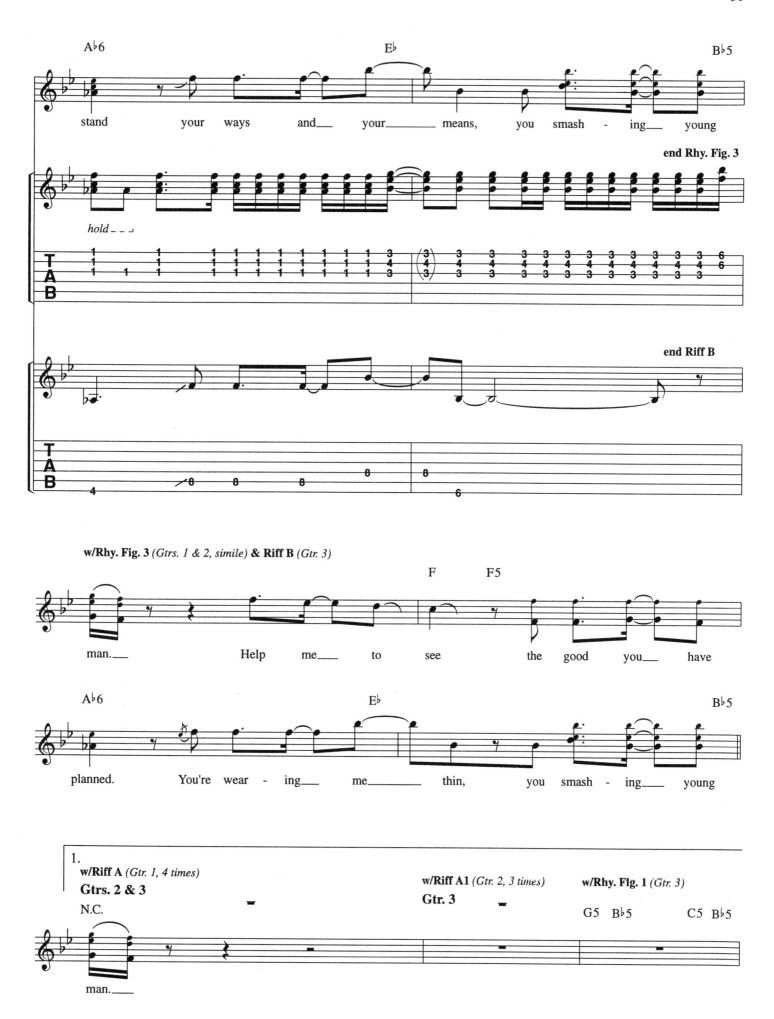

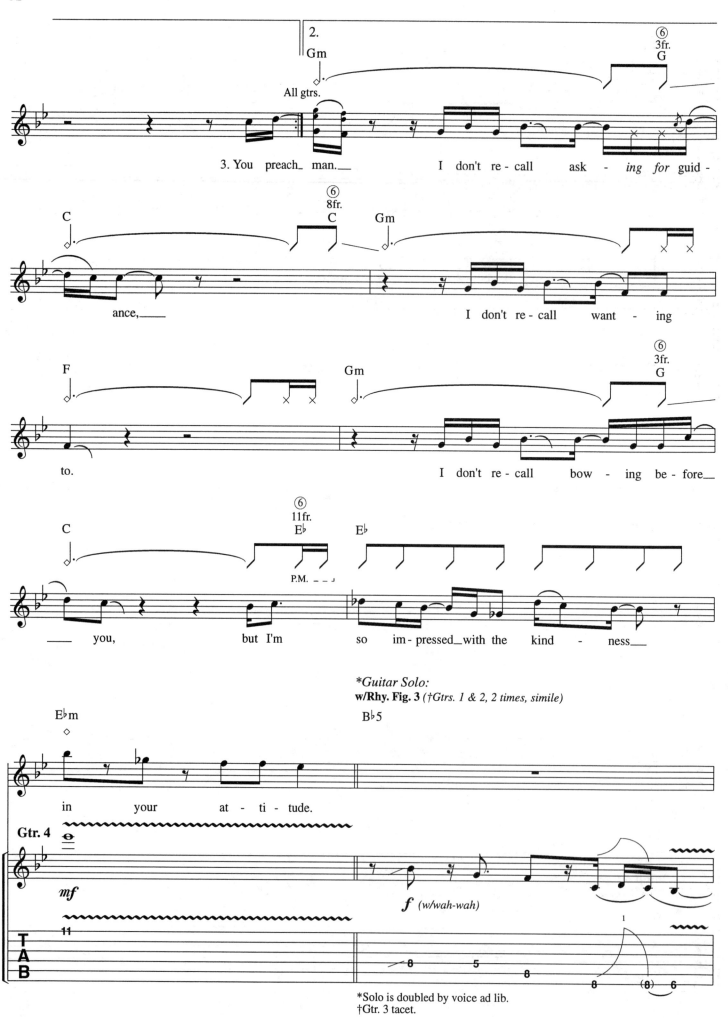

Guitar Solo:
w/Rhy. Fig. 3 (*†Gtrs. 1 & 2, 2 times, simile*)

*Solo is doubled by voice ad lib.
†Gtr. 3 tacet.

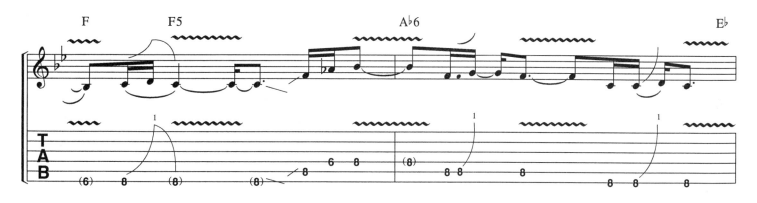

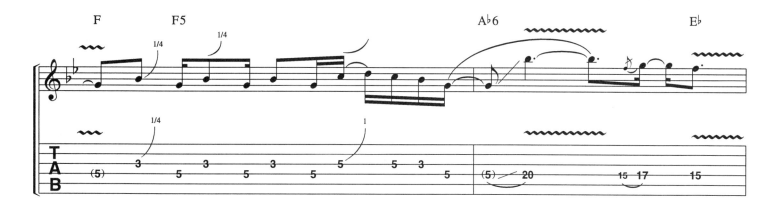

Chorus:
w/Rhy. Fig. 3 *(Gtrs. 1 & 2, 4 times, simile)* &
Riff B *(Gtr. 3, 4 times)*

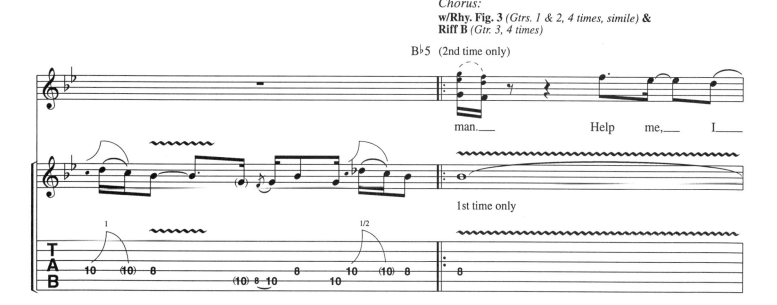

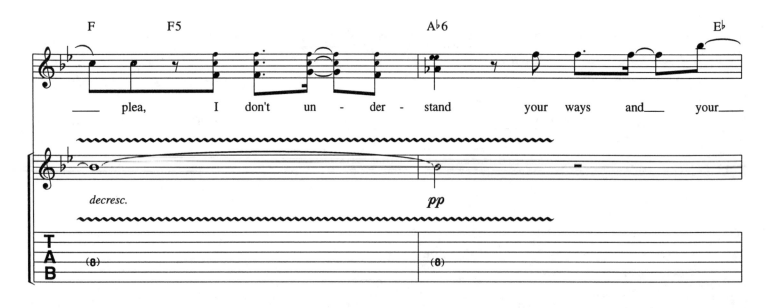

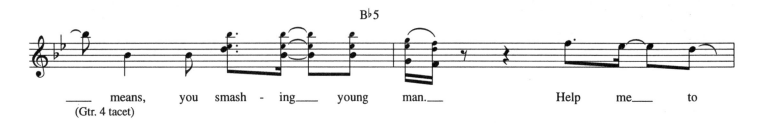

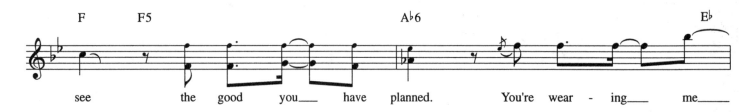

Verse 3:
You preach synthetic-like
And peace is an oversight.
It's nothing to ignite
Your self-lit spotlight.
Hey, I hope you're feeling
A little special now.
Hey, I want to tell you
I think you're special now.
(To Chorus:)

DECEMBER

Music and Lyrics by
ED ROLAND

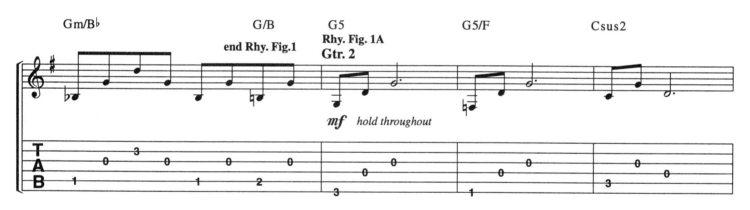

Verse:
w/Rhy. Figs. 1 (Gtr. 1) & 1A (Gtr. 2) Both 4 times

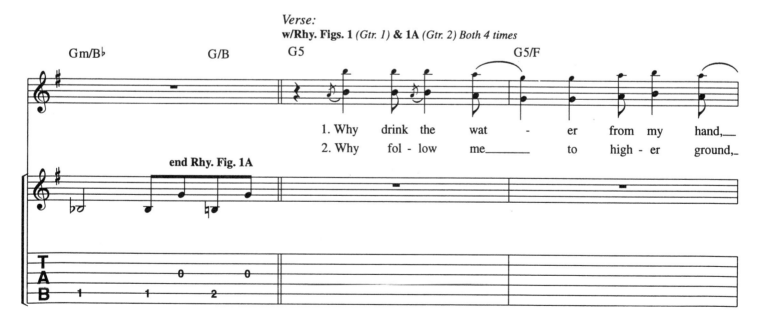

1. Why drink the wat - er from my hand,___
2. Why fol - low me___ to high - er ground,___

December - 5 - 1

WHERE THE RIVER FLOWS

Music and Lyrics by
ED ROLAND

Gtrs. 1 & 2 tuned:

⑥ = C ③ = F
⑤ = G ② = A
④ = C ① = D

Moderately ♩ = 124
Intro:

*D5   E5 D5 F5   D5 E5 D5 F5   D5   E5 D5 F5

Gtrs. 1 & 2

*Song sounds in the key of C.

D5 E5 D5 F5   𝄋 *Verse:* G5

1. Give me___ a mo - ment,___
2. I'll give___ you an - swers___
3. Make no___ more wish - es,___

D5 E5 F5 D5   E5 D5 F5

got to get___ this a - weight up off___ my chest.___
to the ques - tions you have yet___ to ask.___
all of___ my pa - tience has___ been spent.___

Don't feed__ me sor - row,__ pain is__ a
Si - lence__ is beau - ty,__ words they on - ly
Gods of__ the sea - son__ lead me to my

poi - son I__ di - gest.__
com - pli - cate__ the task.__
next in - ci - dent.__

42

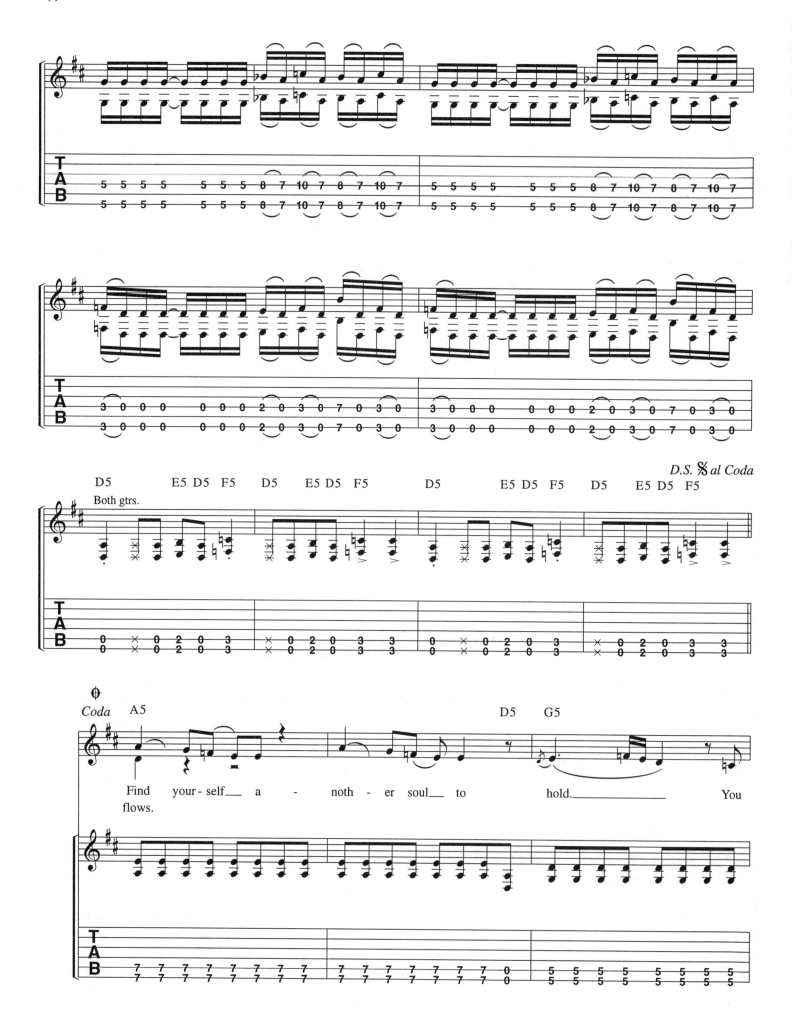

Find your - self___ a - noth - er soul___ to hold._____ You
flows.

GEL

Music and Lyrics by
ED ROLAND

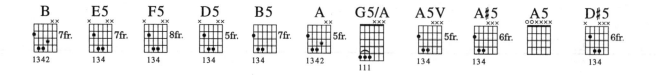

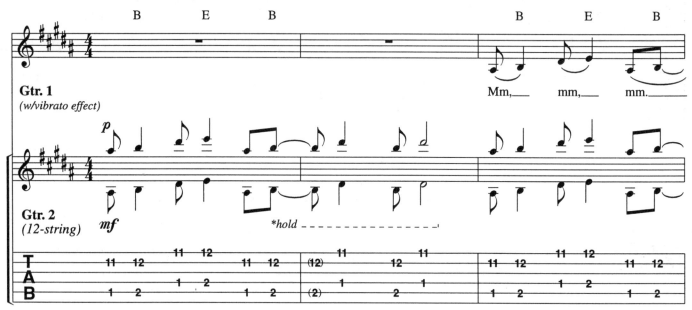

*Applies to both gtrs.

Gel - 8 - 1
PG9536

48

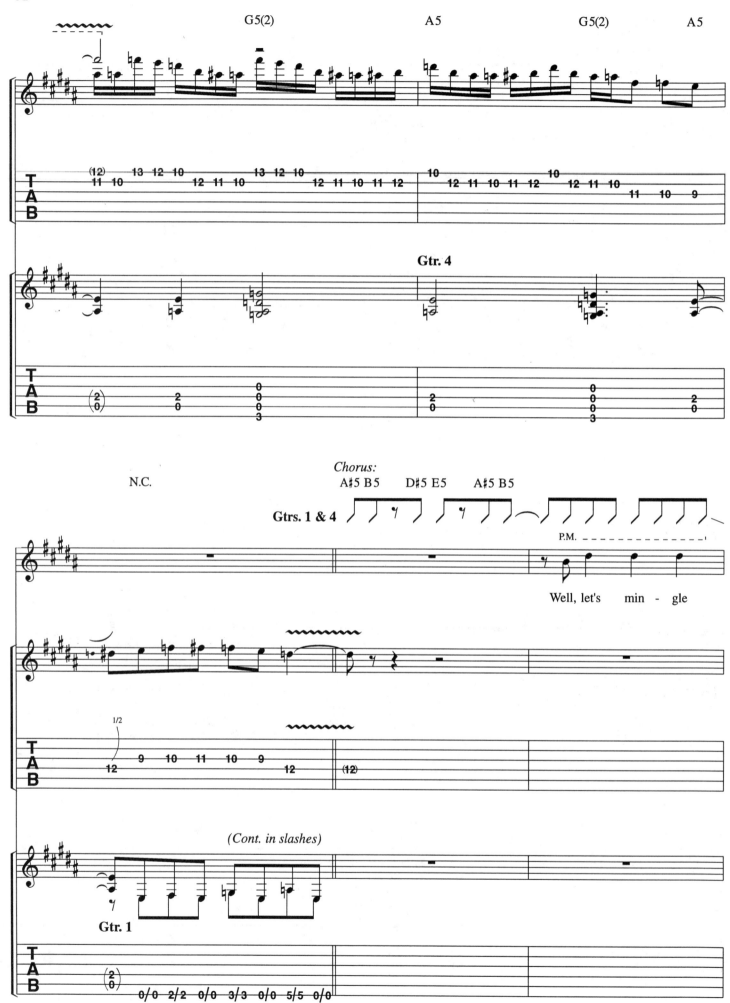

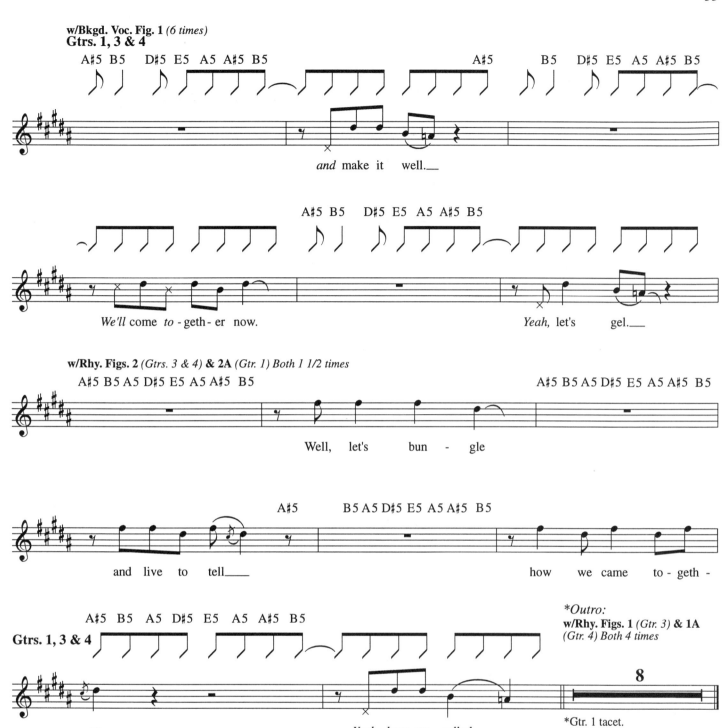

Verse 2:
Clothe me in any fashion.
Glitter to so mundane.
Tell me how you'd love to change me.
Tell me I can stay the same.
Well, I just want to shake us up.
Well, I just want, I just-a want to,
To shake us up.
(To Chorus:)

SHE GATHERS RAIN

Music and Lyrics by
ED ROLAND

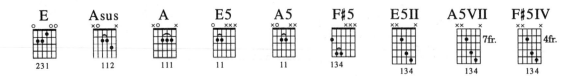

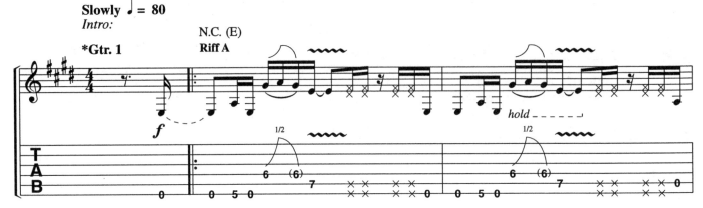

*2nd time doubled by Gtr. 2. 1st note tied 1st time only.

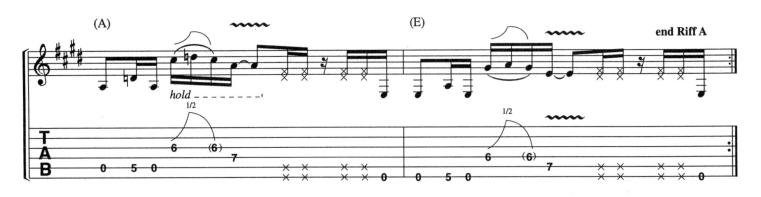

1. To - day__ she dress - es   for the change__ she fac - es
2. *See additional lyrics*

now.__

She Gathers Rain - 8 - 1
PG9536

56

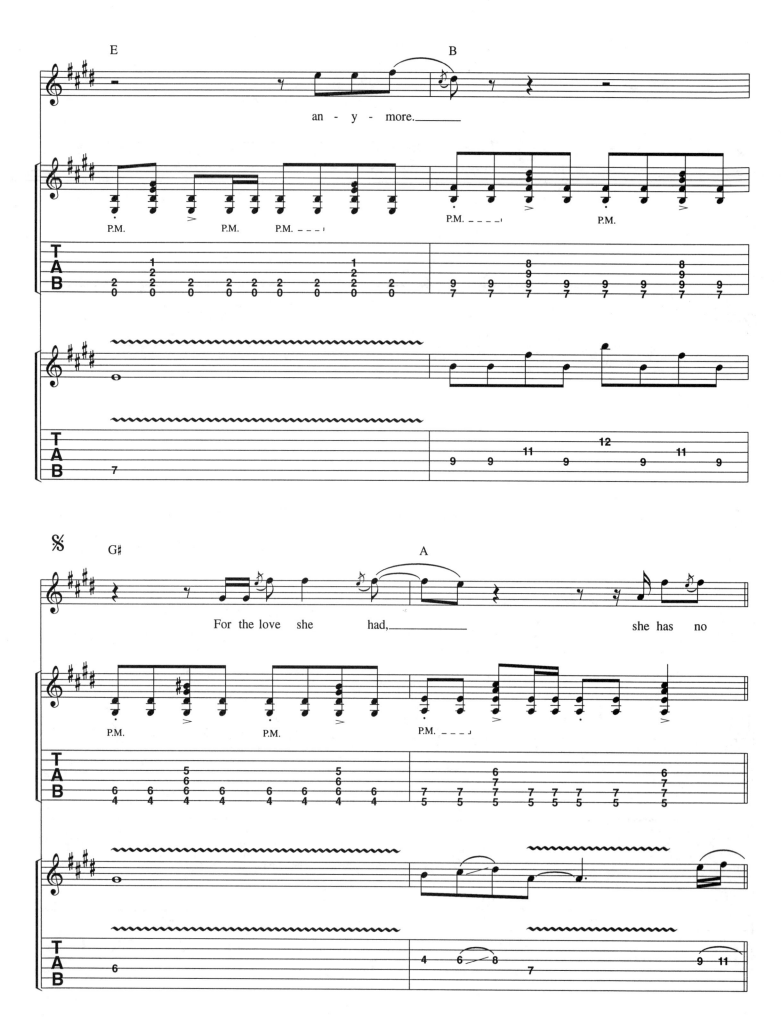

58

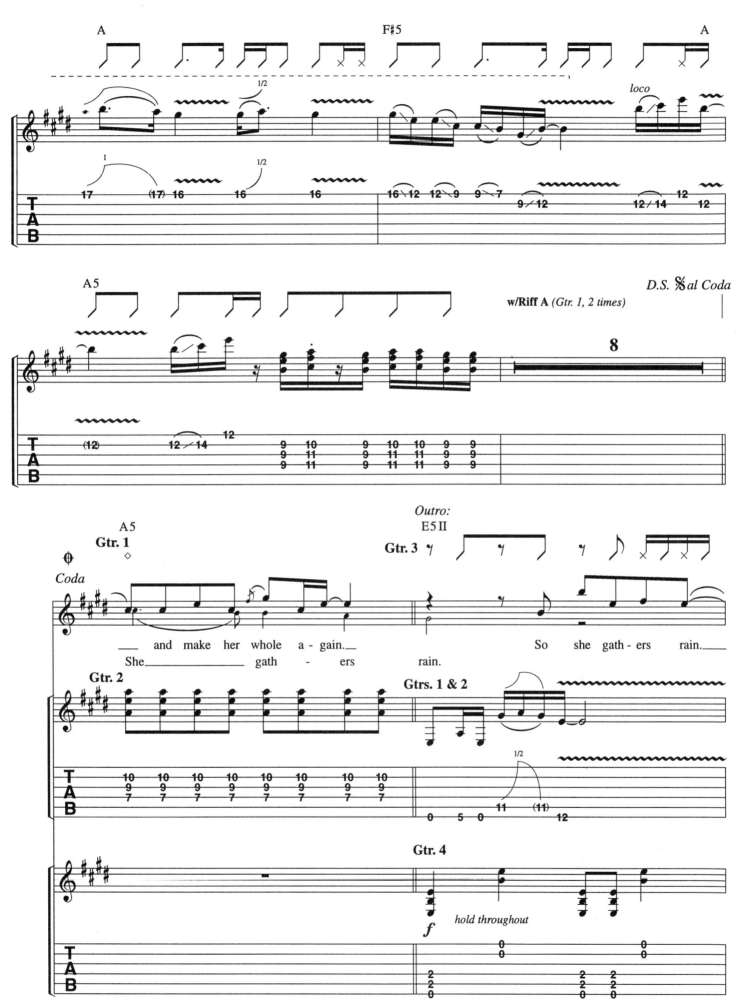

60

Verse 2:
Her imagination
Has started stretching wide.
And her new conviction
No longer will she hide.

Pre-Chorus 2:
She's not branded
When the prophets speak words of fire.
The same love she gives, she requires.
(To Chorus:)

WHEN THE WATER FALLS

Music and Lyrics by
ED ROLAND

When The Water Falls - 8 - 1
PG9536

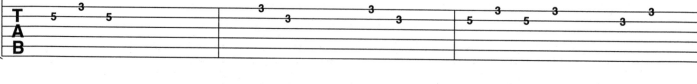

when the wa - ter___ falls?___

end Rhy. Fig. 3

end Rhy. Fig. 3a

2. Though I

Verse 2:
Though I think her subjects could run far and wide.
She has centered on the topic of the sky.
(To Pre-Chorus:)

COLLECTION OF GOODS

Music and Lyrics by
ED ROLAND

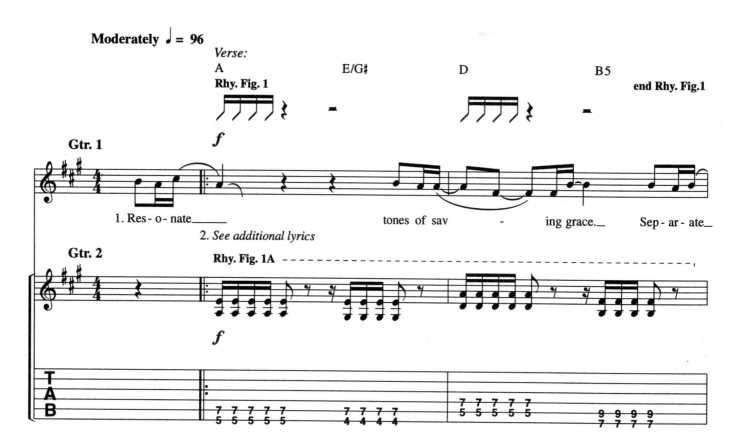

Collection of Goods - 6 - 1
PG9536

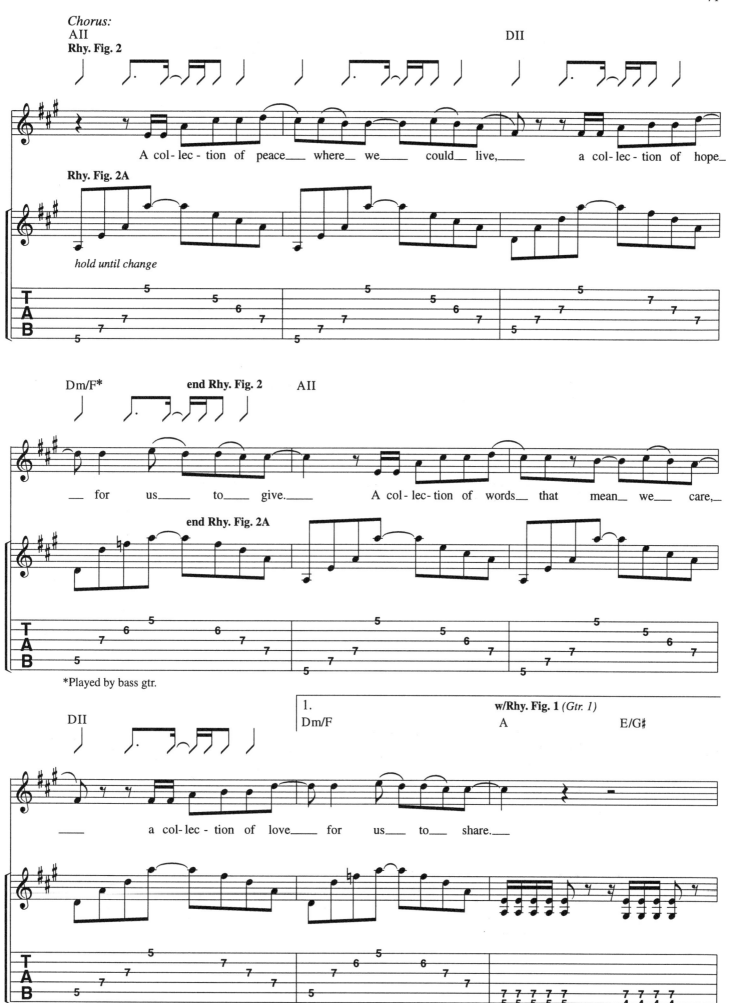

72

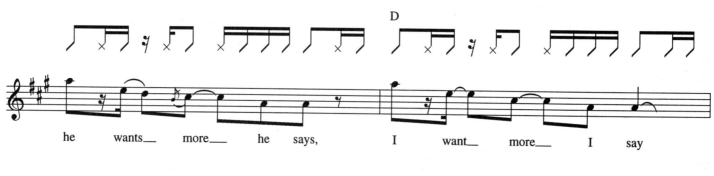

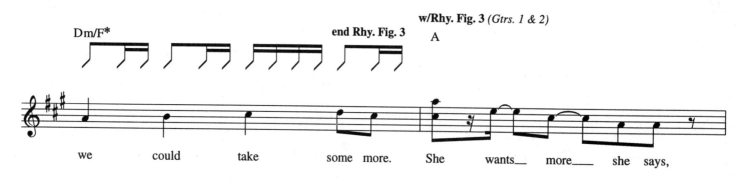

Collection of Goods - 6 - 3
PG9536

74

A col-lec-tion of peace__ where__ we__ could__ live,__ a col-lec-tion of hope__

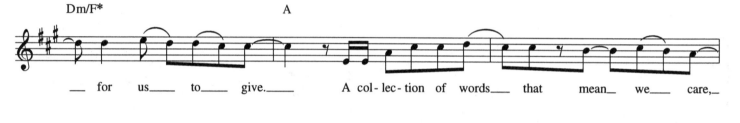

__ for us__ to__ give.__ A col-lec-tion of words__ that mean__ we__ care,__

__ a col-lec-tion of love__ for us__ to__ share.__ __ for us__ to__ share.__

She wants__ more__ she said, he wants__ more__ he says,

Verse 2:
Recognize all equality.
Vocalize solidarity.
Exercise your tranquility.
Glamourize all of love's needs.
(To Chorus:)

BLEED

Music and Lyrics by
ED ROLAND

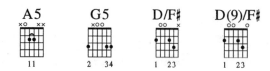

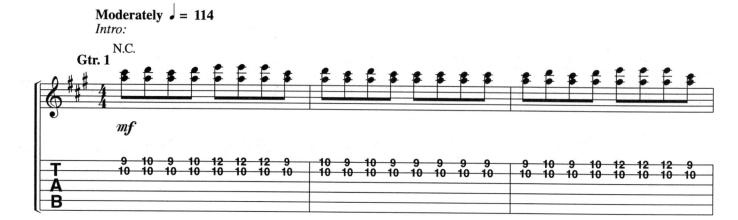

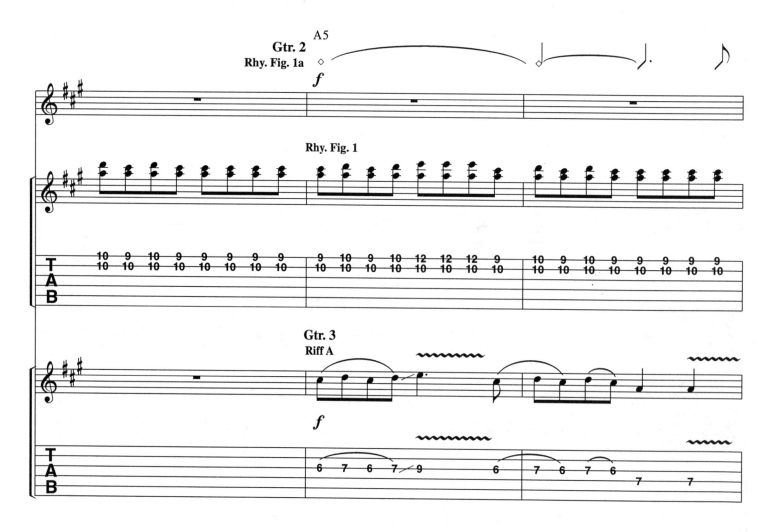

Bleed - 8 - 1
PG9536

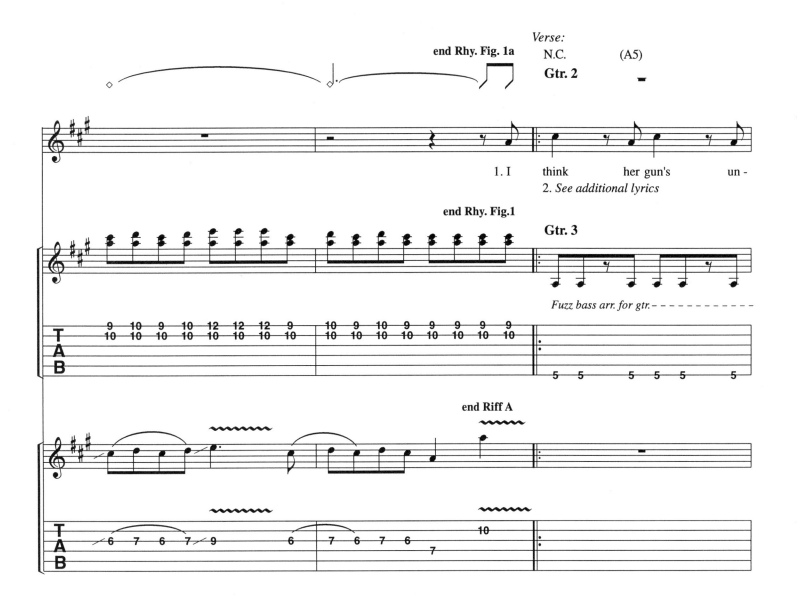

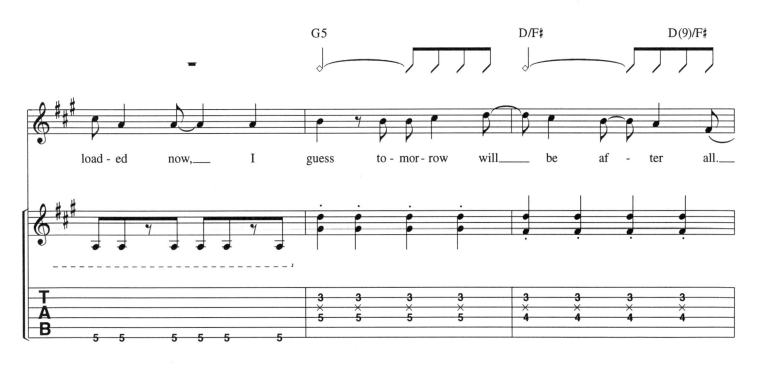

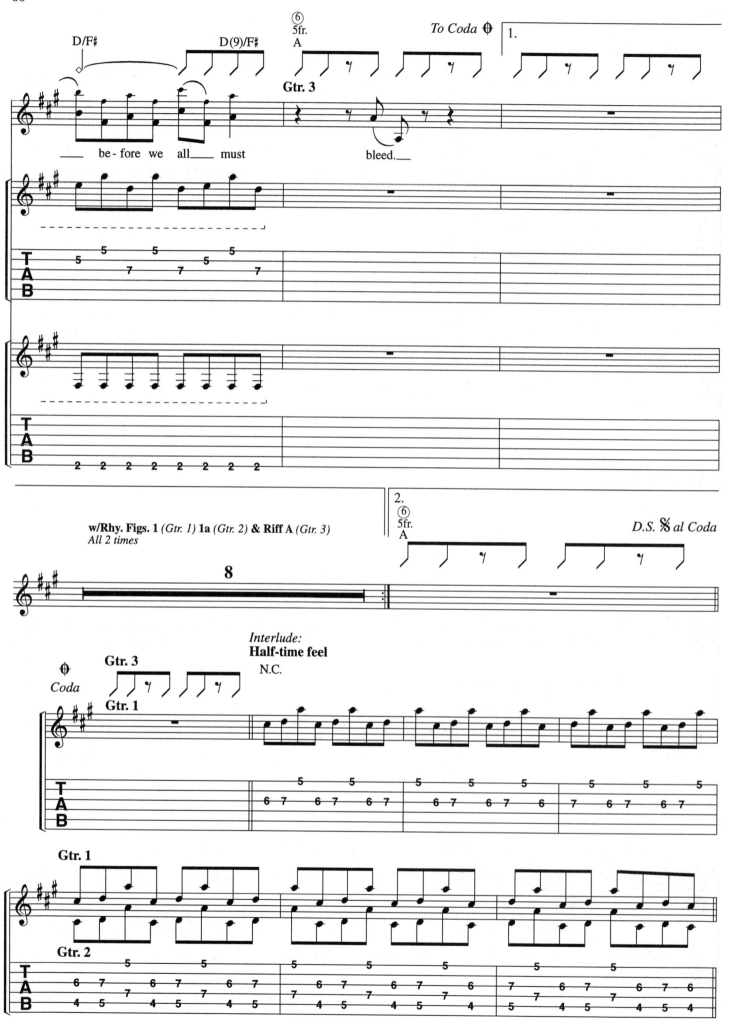

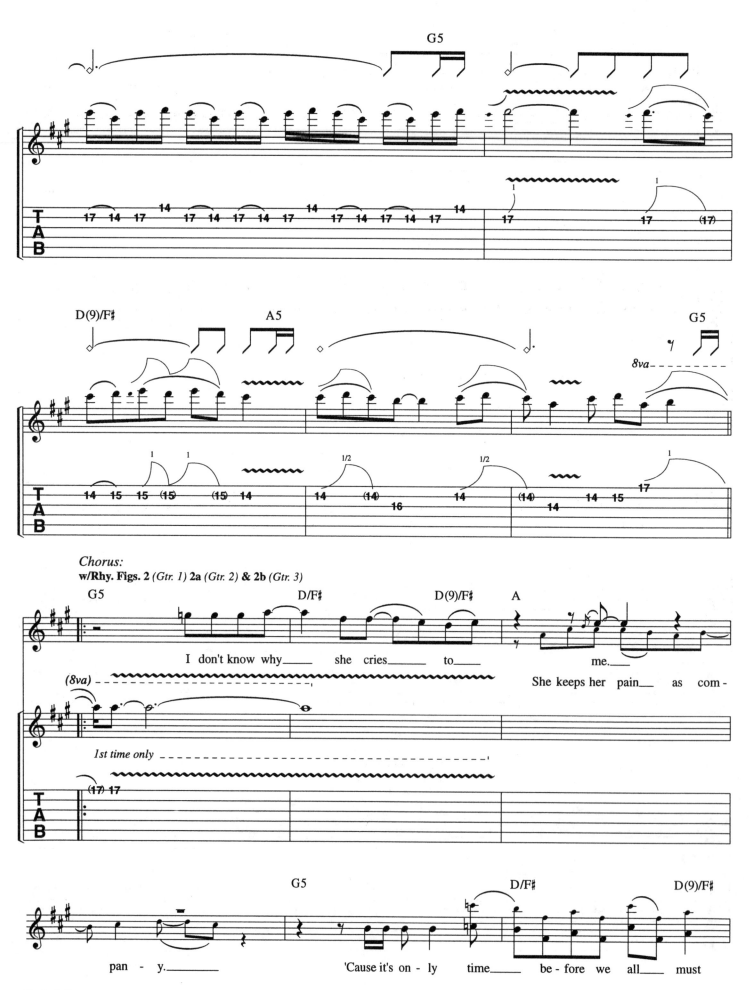

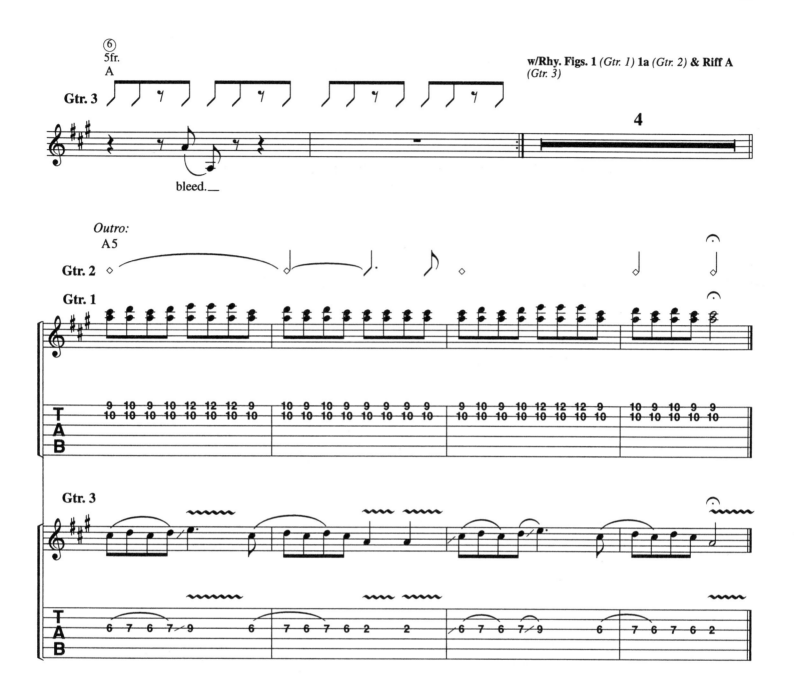

Verse 2:
Mirrors of her memory
Reflect nothing with
Each word she says.
Her views have got
Me spinning 'round.
I think she's burning
Altars in my head.
(To Chorus:)

REUNION

Music and Lyrics by
ED ROLAND

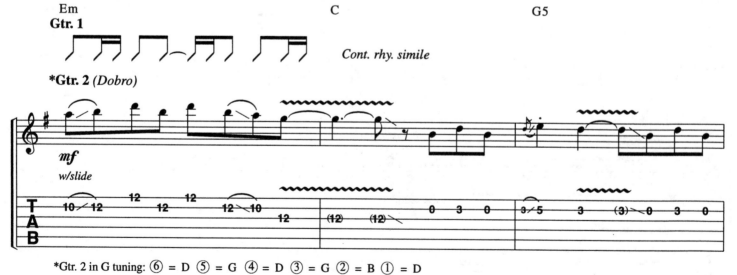

*Gtr. 2 in G tuning: ⑥ = D ⑤ = G ④ = D ③ = G ② = B ① = D

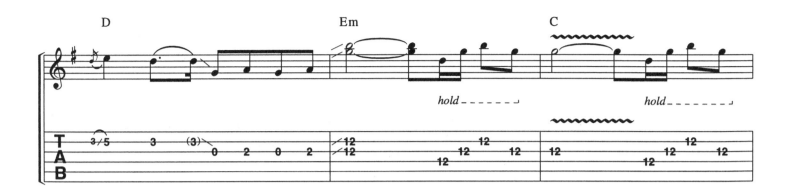

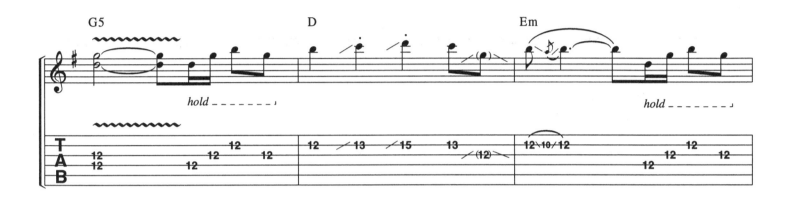

w/Rhy. Fig. 1

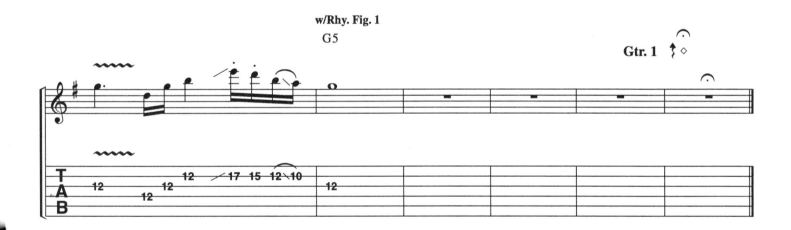

Verse 2:
Change has been.
Change will be.
Time will tell,
Then time will ease.
Now my curtain has been drawn.
And my heart can go
Where my heart does belong.
I'm going home.
(To Guitar Solo:)

GUITAR TAB GLOSSARY **

TABLATURE EXPLANATION

READING TABLATURE: Tablature illustrates the six strings of the guitar. Notes and chords are indicated by the placement of fret numbers on a given string(s).

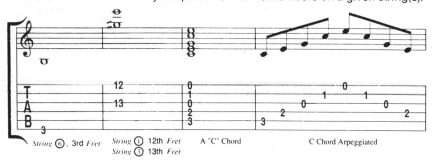

String ⑥, 3rd Fret   *String ① 12th Fret*   A "C" Chord   C Chord Arpeggiated
String ③ 13th Fret

BENDING NOTES

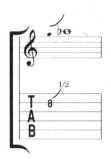

HALF STEP: Play the note and bend string one half step.*

WHOLE STEP: Play the note and bend string one whole step.

PREBEND AND RELEASE: Bend the string, play it, then release to the original note.

RHYTHM SLASHES

STRUM INDICA-TIONS: Strum with indicated rhythm. The chord voicings are found on the first page of the transcription underneath the song title.

INDICATING SINGLE NOTES USING RHYTHM SLASHES: Very often single notes are incorporated into a rhythm part. The note name is indicated above the rhythm slash with a fret number and a string indication.

*A half step is the smallest interval in Western music; it is equal to one fret. A whole step equals two frets.

**By Kenn Chipkin and Aaron Stang

ARTICULATIONS

HAMMER ON: Play lower note, then "hammer on" to higher note with another finger. Only the first note is attacked.

PULL OFF: Play higher note, then "pull off" to lower note with another finger. Only the first note is attacked.

LEGATO SLIDE: Play note and slide to the following note. (Only first note is attacked).

PALM MUTE: The note or notes are muted by the palm of the pick hand by lightly touching the string(s) near the bridge.

ACCENT: Notes or chords are to be played with added emphasis.

DOWN STROKES AND UPSTROKES: Notes or chords are to be played with either a downstroke (⊓) or upstroke (∨) of the pick.

© 1990 Beam Me Up Music
c/o CPP/Belwin, Inc. Miami, Florida 33014